Secrets
Jesus told

Story by Penny Frank

Illustrated by John Haysom

THE LION
STORY BIBLE

37

TRING · BATAVIA · SYDNEY

T he Bible tells us
how God sent his Son Jesus to show
us what God is like and how we can
belong to God's kingdom.
Jesus enjoyed telling people some
of God's secrets. You can find them in
your own Bible, in the Gospels of
Matthew and Luke.

Copyright © 1987 Lion Publishing

Published by
Lion Publishing plc
Icknield Way, Tring, Herts, England
ISBN 0 85648 762 7
Lion Publishing Corporation
1705 Hubbard Avenue, Batavia,
Illinois 60510, USA
ISBN 0 85648 762 7
Albatross Books Pty Ltd
PO Box 320, Sutherland, NSW 2232, Australia
ISBN 0 86760 547 2

First edition 1987

Printed and bound in Belgium

British Library Cataloguing in Publication Data

Frank, Penny
Secrets Jesus told.—(The Lion Story Bible; 37)
1. Jesus Christ—Parables—Juvenile literature
I. Title   II. Haysom, John
226'.809505   BT376
ISBN 0-85648-762-7

Library of Congress Cataloging-in-Publication Data

Frank, Penny.
Secrets Jesus told.
(The Lion Story Bible; 37)
1. Jesus Christ—Teachings—Juvenile literature. [1. Jesus Christ—Teachings]
I. Haysom, John, ill. II. Title. III. Series: Frank, Penny. Lion Story Bible; 37.
BS2416.F73 1987   232.9'54
86-15324
ISBN 0-85648-762-7

One day so many people came to listen
to Jesus that there was no room left on
the beach by Lake Galilee. Jesus was
being pushed further and further back,
towards the water.

So he climbed into his friends' boat
and they pushed it a little way out onto
the lake. Then everyone could hear.

'Well,' Jesus said to them, across the still,
clear water. 'What would you like to
hear about today?

'Have you come just for fun, to watch people being healed and to listen to stories? Or do you really want to learn more about God? Listen, and I'll tell you some of the secrets of God's kingdom.

'God's kingdom is like a little mustard seed — so tiny you can hardly see it. A farmer takes the seed and plants it in his field. You wouldn't know it was there.

'But, when it grows tall, it spreads out so many branches that the birds build their nests in it.

'That's what God's kingdom is like. It seems small now, but it will grow and grow.

'God's kingdom is like yeast. It looks quite dead, like a little lump of clay.

'Then it goes into the bowl with the flour and water. They are stirred up together until no one can see where the yeast has gone.

'But when the dough is left in the warm it swells and swells — all because of that little lump of yeast.

'That's what God's kingdom is like, quietly working, but able to change everything.

'God's kingdom is like treasure, buried in a field. One day a man is busy digging, when his spade bangs against something hard. He can hardly believe that he has found treasure.

'He covers it up and keeps it secret. He sells everything he owns to get enough money to buy that field. Then the treasure is his.

'That is what God's kingdom is like. It's worth more than everything else we have.

'I'll tell you another secret,' Jesus said. 'God really wants you to belong to his kingdom.

'Have you ever lost some money? If you did, you would search the whole house to find it!

'And when you found it, you would run and tell everyone, you would be so happy.

'That is how it is with God's kingdom, too. Each of you is like a lost coin, and God is very glad when you are found.

'You don't ever need to be afraid,' Jesus said. 'Each one of you is very important to God. He notices when a tiny bird is hurt, and you matter much more than the birds.

'God even knows how many hairs are growing on your head!'

The people laughed. The children looked at each other. Their hair was thick and dark. Imagine God knowing that!

'You can understand some of God's secrets just by looking around you,' Jesus said. 'See that tree over there? You can tell it is a good tree, can't you? Its branches are bent over with the heavy crop of fruit.

'But that tree on the other side of the wall is bad. Its branches are thin and weak and the fruit is not worth picking. In the same way you can tell if a person is good or bad by what they do and say.

'I won't always be here with you,' Jesus said. 'While I'm away, I want you to use your time well. You are all good at different things, so don't be lazy. Fill your days by being busy for me.

'There was once a man who went on a journey. Before he went, he gave each of his servants some money. One had a lot; another had just a little. But he expected all of them to use the money they had to earn more.

'One day,' Jesus said, 'I will come back again. Remember that secret when everything seems difficult. Then everyone will know that I am the King God has put in charge of his kingdom.

'Trumpets will sound. The angels will gather the people who belong to God's kingdom from every part of the earth. So make sure you are ready!

'There are two roads and they lead to
different places.

'The wide road is smooth and easy to
travel on. But don't choose that road,
because it leads to Satan's kingdom.

'The road you need,' said Jesus, 'is a narrow road and it's hard to find. It is difficult to travel on. But that is the road to choose, because it leads to God's kingdom. Make sure you find it.

'That is the greatest secret of all.'

The Lion Story Bible is made up of 52 individual stories for young readers, building up an understanding of the Bible as one story — God's story — a story for all time and all people.

The New Testament section (numbers 31–52) covers the life and teaching of God's Son, Jesus. The stories are about the people he met, what he did and what he said. Almost all we know about the life of Jesus is recorded in the four Gospels — Matthew, Mark, Luke and John. The word gospel means 'good news'.

The last four stories in this section are about the first Christians, who started to tell others the 'good news', as Jesus had commanded them — a story which continues today all over the world.

Secrets Jesus told, the parables (stories with a special meaning) about God's kingdom, comes from the New Testament. The mustard seed, yeast and hidden treasure are from Matthew's Gospel, chapter 13. The lost coin is from Luke, chapter 15; the tree and its fruit from Luke, chapter 6; the 'talents' from Matthew, chapter 25; the two roads from Matthew, chapter 7.

In this life each of us is free to choose the road we travel on, but the two roads go in different directions. God wants us to choose the way that leads to his kingdom so that we may enjoy it with him when Jesus returns as King.

The next book in the series, number 38: *The story of the good Samaritan*, is one of Jesus' best-known stories.